MW01697541

making wise CHOICES

BY JOEL OSTEEN

Joel Osteen Ministries
P.O. Box 4600
Houston, TX 77210
888-870-7034
JoelOsteen.com

All Bible verses are from the New International Version unless otherwise noted.

Introduction

Life is really a series of choices – have you noticed? We make hundreds of choices every single day, many of them without even thinking. We choose what to wear, where to go, what to say and how to act. Of course, some of our choices are trivial and don't have any lasting impact on our lives – but I think you'd be amazed how many other choices you and I make that can greatly affect our future.

For example, you choose your thoughts every day. You choose which ones you'll dwell on, and which ones you'll ignore. You choose your attitude and who you're going to associate with. You choose who you'll listen to, and how you see yourself.

Choices are extremely important. That's because *the quality of your life will be determined by the quality of your choices.* You say, "Joel, I don't know if I believe that." Well friends, it's true. You are what you are today because of the choices you have made in the past. And what you'll be in the future will be a result of the choices you're making right now – today.

God has a great plan and purpose for your life. The Bible says that God saw you before you were even formed in your mother's womb (Psalm 139:13), and that He has planned out all of your days for good and not for evil (Jeremiah 29:11). The Apostle Paul said that God wants to do much more for us than we can even ask or think (Ephesians 3:20)!

Then why do so many people struggle when God is surely for us? Why are you in debt today, or living in fear, or experiencing trouble in your relationships? Why does it seem at times that life is just one big mess? I'm convinced it has a whole lot to do with our choices.

I believe that if you and I can learn to make the right choices, we will live the life of victory that God has in store for us.

No matter what you're going through right now, I can tell you with confidence that God has a great future planned for you. No matter what is in your past, He is holding out hope for a new beginning... and you can start to realize it by learning to make wise choices.

Choose to Heed God's Wisdom

Every believer can learn to walk in the wisdom God gives His people. You don't have to blindly follow the devil anymore. The Bible says that God has given you a spirit of wisdom. Proverbs 2:6 says, "The Lord grants wisdom." In other words, God gives good sense to the godly! He shows us how to distinguish right from wrong, and how to make the right decision every time.

Even though we may blame others for the choices we make, most of the setbacks we suffer in life are not caused by other people – or even by the devil. They are simply a result of us refusing to listen to godly wisdom and allowing the flesh to have its own way. You see, the devil gets more credit than he deserves! The Bible says that if you are in Christ, you are a new creature, and the old things that used to control you don't have power over you anymore.

Our flesh is naturally ruled by our emotions – by what we feel, what we think and what we want. But the Bible says the Spirit of God should lead us instead. Anyone who lives on the shallow level of doing whatever feels right will go from one disaster in life to the next. But the man or woman who listens to and heeds the voice of godly wisdom will prosper.

This is what the Living Bible says in Proverbs 8 about wisdom: *"Can't you hear the voice of wisdom calling out to you? She is standing at every fork in the road. Listen to what she says, 'Let me give you understanding. Let me give you good sense. I have important information for you. Everything I say is right and true. My words are plain and clear to anyone with half a mind if it is only open."*

Notice that wisdom stands "at every fork in the road." In other words, every time you and I come to a crossroads or a place of decision where we could go one way or another, God's wisdom will be there, crying out to us and trying to tell us the right decision to make.

Friends, you and I can make the right decisions in life if we'll just start listening to God's wisdom and stop being ruled by our emotions. I like that same passage from Proverbs in *The Message* translation. *"Listen you idiots! Learn good sense. Listen you blockheads! Shape up! I'm telling you how to live at your best."* Now that's pretty frank – but it's saying that God's wisdom is constantly trying to break through our hard heads to help us make the right decisions, and choose the right path.

If you're tempted to be unfaithful to your mate, you need to listen to the voice of godly wisdom, and consider the long-term consequences. Wisdom would say that to gratify your flesh in the moment could end up destroying your family. If you're tempted to spend money you don't have to make yourself feel better, wisdom would say don't let your emotions put you in debt. Teenagers, when you're caught up in the heat of the moment and you feel your passions taking over, wisdom would say to stop before the price of your decision is an unwanted pregnancy or a broken heart.

These are hard things to consider, and even harder things to do – but this is where the rubber meets the road! This is the kind of truth that is going to help you reach your full potential in life.

Friends, all the faith in the world can't substitute for listening to God's wisdom and making wise choices. And you'll never have prosperity if you don't know how to say "no" to your flesh and your emotions and "yes" to God's wisdom. Proverbs 3:16 says, "Wisdom brings us riches, honor and a long life," so let me challenge you to learn to yield to wisdom. Then you will live the overcoming life of victory that God has in store for you.

Choose to Set Right Priorities

We live in a very hectic and fast-paced society. People are always rushing here and there to meet a deadline, pick up the kids, meet a friend after work or get to their next appointment. It seems like everybody's busy. Like everybody's in a hurry. Sometimes we may feel like we're going ninety miles an hour – but not making a whole lot of progress!

But some of the busiest people I know are not busy fulfilling their destiny. Instead, they're living stressed out, uptight, frustrated lives. And one of the main reasons they're stressed and unproductive is that *they don't have their priorities in order.*

Did you know that it's nearly impossible to make wise choices when our priorities are out of line? It's true. People who try to please everyone and are afraid to say no tend to live in a whirlwind. And that's not good.

One of the enemy's favorite tricks is to deceive us into living in the extremes. Our enemy, the devil, is happy to see us always busy, always working, always going. That's because excess is his playground. He would love to keep us all so busy doing a thousand different things that we miss out on the main thing God really wants us to do.

The Bible says in I Peter 5:8 that God wants us to live well balanced lives, but to do that, we've got to get our priorities in order. We've got to take stock and determine what's truly important, then set some boundaries for ourselves and honor them.

Friends, if you are too busy to pray, too busy to come to church, too busy to take care of your marriage or too busy to spend time with your family – you're too busy! It may be time to "prune away" some of the areas of excess that are stealing your time and robbing you of God's abundant life.

I learned a lesson about pruning in my own front yard. Victoria and I have crepe myrtle trees planted along our driveway at home. Every year they blossom with bright, beautiful flowers and we love seeing them. But one year, I noticed the crepe myrtles didn't bloom. So I called the nursery and asked what had happened.

The first thing the people asked me was "Did you prune them back in the fall?" I said no, I hadn't done that – in fact, I didn't know you *had* to prune them! They went on to explain to me that unless I pruned our crepe myrtles to get rid of the old growth, the plant would use all its energy trying to nurture the excess, and not produce any flowers. In other words – the excess foliage would "steal" energy from any new growth!

It's really the same way with all of us. When we don't keep our lives pruned, and we don't get rid of the excess areas that aren't fruitful, then those areas of excess are going to consume our time and our energy – and we're going to end up living very mediocre lives.

God never told us to get busy. He told us to be fruitful. And there's a big difference in being busy and in bearing fruit. The word "fruitful" actually means, "to produce in abundance that which is profitable." When we're fruitful, we're productive in ways that are profitable – and we're not exhausted, we're energized! We're doing things that are rewarding and fulfilling, and those things bring us joy.

So let me ask you a question: Are you being busy, or are you being fruitful? If you're not sure, it's time to take a look at your life and ask: "What areas of my life are most important? Where do I experience joy? What things produce fulfillment in me and bear fruit in my life and in the lives of others?"

Friends, it's a new day, a new season – and God wants to do a new thing. (Isaiah 43:17-18)

We can't afford to listen to the lies of the enemy. We can't let our pride get in the way. And we can't even be overly concerned about what other people will think. We've got to do what we know God wants us to do down in our heart of hearts. Like the writer of Hebrews said, "Let us strip off every weight. Let us throw aside every unnecessary encumbrance that entangles us and let us run with patience the race that is set before us." (Hebrews 12:1-2)

When we do that, we'll experience new levels of growth, and our lives are sure to blossom with the good things of God!

Choose to Walk in Integrity

If you and I are going to experience God's best, we're going to have to live open and honest lives and go the extra mile to do what's right. That means *choosing to walk in integrity.*

Integrity takes the high road. Integrity does the right thing, regardless of whether anyone is watching. People of integrity are true to their word. They don't need a legal contract to bind them to an agreement. They do what they say they will do because they have given their word!

When you have integrity you say what you mean and mean what you say. You don't have any hidden agendas or ulterior motives. People don't have to wonder what you really mean. You tell them. You treat others the way you would like to be treated yourself, and you are the same person in private that you are in public.

People of integrity stand out today because we are experiencing an integrity crisis. Lying and cheating are common practices. The lines between right and wrong have become blurred. Personal standards have sunk to an all time low as people pursue any pleasure and take any shortcut to success.

But God is after something different. He's looking for people with the will to walk in integrity – people who will do what's right when everyone else is doing what's wrong. So if you and I are going to experience the life God has in store for us, we're going to have to be willing to be different. We're going to have to go against the grain and choose integrity.

My dad went to be with the Lord in 1999, but when I think about Daddy's life, two things come to mind: first, he was a man of great love. He always believed the best in people. And second, he was a man of great integrity. He was the same at home as he was behind the pulpit. My dad was a man who kept his word – to his children, to his family and to his church.

I believe my dad operated that way because he knew that God sees everything we do and the motives *behind* what we do.

I worked with him behind the scenes for 17 years at Lakewood Church, and I can tell you firsthand that he treated people right. He handled finances right. He made wise decisions. I know in my heart that Lakewood is stronger than ever today because John Osteen laid that foundation of integrity, and God has blessed it.

Proverbs 11:3 says, "The integrity of the upright shall guide them." Friends, I want to challenge you to live a life of integrity. Don't compromise in the little areas. Do the right thing, even when no one is watching. Be a person of excellence. One day you and I will stand before God and give an account of what we've done. Our integrity and our desire to live lives that honor God will be pleasing sacrifices to Him.

I don't always know the right decisions to make in life. I don't always know what's best for Lakewood Church. But I do know that if I'll keep my heart pure and take the high road by choosing the way of integrity, God will guide me and protect me and keep me from stumbling. And if He'll do it for me, you can believe He'll do it for you as well. Then you'll live that life of overcoming victory that rightly belongs to every child of God.

Choose to Wait for God's Timing

Have you ever heard the saying "timing is everything?" Well, it may not be everything, but it sure is important! And when you and I want to make wise choices in life, timing is critical – especially *God's timing.*

God has put dreams and desires in each one of our hearts. We all have things that we're hoping for and praying for. And the Bible says in the book of I John 5:14-15 that if we ask in faith, according to God's will, He will hear us and answer those prayers.

What it doesn't say is *when.* I've noticed that God never puts a time frame on His promises to answer us. He never tells us the hour or the day He will bring our dreams to pass. He doesn't say "If you pray in faith, I'll get back to you in two weeks time." No. He doesn't say "I'll get you out of debt in a month," or "I'll restore your marriage in six weeks."

As much as we would like to know *when,* God doesn't spell out specific times for the answers to our prayers. He simply promises us that if we'll put our total trust and confidence in Him – and refuse to worry or try to make things happen in our own strength – He will give us His answer – in the right way and at the right time.

The tough part is waiting for Him to do just that.

I'm convinced that many people today are stepping outside of God's will and settling for second best simply because they're too impatient to wait. They're in such a hurry that they try to make things happen in their own strength. Because they don't understand God's timing, they think He is not working at all – and they couldn't be further from the truth.

When you boil it all down, unwillingness to wait for God's timing is nothing more than a lack of trust. Scripture says in Habakkuk 2:3 that "the vision is for an appointed time. Though it tarry, wait earnestly for it, for it will surely come."

Friends, God has appointed a time to bring your dreams to pass. He has appointed a specific time to answer your prayers. It's the right time. It's the best time. It's the time worth waiting for. So when you have prayed, when you have sought God's answer, when you are seeking direction from Him and not relying on your own strength, you can expectantly enter into the rest of God and know beyond a shadow of a doubt that He is going to see it through.

Maybe you're single today and praying for God to bring you a mate. You don't have to force that to happen. Wait for God's perfect timing, and don't get frustrated because your friends are all married and you can't even get a date! Don't rush ahead of God or settle for second best. Just be patient and trust Him, and in due season God will answer your prayers.

Maybe you're married, but praying for your husband or your wife to be born again. You don't have to shove the Gospel down your mate's throat, or try to make him or her feel guilty for not coming to church. You're not responsible for your mate's salvation. No, you're responsible for your own faithfulness. You are to let your light shine, and treat your partner with love and respect. The rest is up to God. In His perfect timing, He will surely accomplish that which concerns you.

The Bible is full of stories of those who waited faithfully on God. God gave Moses a dream that he would one day deliver the children of Israel from their slavery in

Egypt. First he tried to make it happen in his own strength, but that was disaster. Then he learned to wait on God and after 40 years on the backside of the desert, God said, "Moses, I believe you're ready. It's time to move out."

God gave Joseph a dream, too. He showed him how one day he'd rule over all of Egypt, and his own brothers would bow down to him. Joseph didn't realize that dream overnight, though. He was sold into slavery and falsely accused and forgotten – and for fourteen years he waited. But Joseph never gave up. He never got bitter. He trusted God, and he waited for God's timing. And God supernaturally turned Joseph's situation around. At age 30, he was promoted to be second-in-command to Pharaoh. His due season arrived because he refused to give up or to compromise. He learned that his God was faithful.

I know some of you have gone through major disappointments in life. You've suffered some big setbacks and gone through long periods of struggle and heartbreak. The enemy's trick is to get you so tired of waiting that you lose hope and give up. He wants you to say, "What's the use? I'll never be happy. I'll never get out of debt. I'll never see my marriage restored. I've done everything I know to do, but nothing's changed."

Don't you believe that old lie!

Jesus said, "He who endures to the end shall receive the prize." God rewards people who don't give up on Him. He shows favor to those with expectant, trusting hearts. So keep taking the high road even when you can't see any end in sight. Keep on being faithful and waiting with a trusting attitude. In due season, you will reap the harvest of the good things of God. (Galatians 6:9) He is in control and He will see you through. All He asks is that you trust Him and enter into His rest. Cease striving, and know that He is God.

Choose Discipline and Self-Control

The apostle Paul wrote to his friends the Galatians that "the fruit of the spirit is self-control." The word he used for "self-discipline" or "self-control" comes from a Greek word that means, "to grip or take hold of." Self-control is literally taking hold of yourself – taking a firm grip on your life.

I've been talking to you about making wise choices in life, and friends, self-control is a wise choice. A person with self-control exercises restraint over his or her thoughts, feelings and emotions in order to achieve a goal.

We have a tendency to think of self-control in a negative way, but self-control is a strong positive! The fruit of the flesh is no-control and it leads us in a downward spiral, but self-control is a tool God has given that can help us accomplish our dreams. In fact, the Bible tells us in II Timothy 1:7 that God has given *every one* of His children a spirit of discipline and self-control!

That means you and I have the ability to "overrule" our feelings. We have the God-given ability to take charge of our lives and do what is right. But discipline and self-control must be exercised. They don't just automatically happen.

I like to lift weights when I go to the gym. Every once in a while, I'll work out on a machine I haven't used before – and in the next couple of days, I discover hurting muscles I never knew I had! It's a little uncomfortable – just like exercising self-control is uncomfortable when we first begin.

Your flesh and my flesh will protest against self-control. Just try to exercise and see. Your flesh is going to say, "What in the world are you doing to me? I can't take this! Just let me have one more hot fudge sundae, or take another lazy nap on the couch. I don't want any pain!"

The Bible says in Hebrews 12:11 that "no discipline at the time seems enjoyable." Discipline or self-control doesn't seem enjoyable because we don't want to be inconvenienced. We don't want to pay the price or endure the pain. We just want to take the easy way out. But I want to challenge you to think ahead. Think beyond the present moment. Remember that the decisions we make today determine where we're going to be later on.

I heard someone put it like this: there are two kinds of pain in life. One is the pain of discipline and the other is the pain of regret. And friends, the pain of discipline weighs ounces, but the pain of regret weighs tons!

I'm not out to make anyone feel bad about their past. All of us have done things we regret. Instead, I want to stir you up and help you get on the right course *today.* God can give you a new beginning!

Yes, it may be a little bit painful to not always have your way. Sure, it hurts at times to keep a good attitude when the bottom falls out. Yes, it's uncomfortable to discipline the flesh and not give in to sinful desires. I'm not saying it will always be easy. I'm not saying there won't be a price to pay. I'm saying the price we pay to be disciplined and exercise self-control is miniscule compared to the price of looking back with regret and longing at what might have been.

Remember, too, that self-control and discipline are learned habits. You'll need to practice them over and over, the way you used to "practice" giving in to the flesh. Good habits, just like bad habits, are formed over time. But now is the time to begin!

Don't let the enemy convince you that you can't change. Don't believe the lie that you can't form new habits. With God's help you can. I don't care how long you've been addicted. I don't care how long you've been lazy. I don't care how long you've had that negative attitude. God has put supernatural power in you to overcome. And the power that is in you is greater than any other power – even the power of addiction.

God is trying to lead and guide us in the way that is best. He is trying to help us reach our full potential. He has placed gifts and talents in each one of us, and He wants us to exercise discipline and self-control so that those good things He's planted can grow.

Are you ready to "get a good grip" on your life and begin to exercise self-control? Are you ready to become the man or woman God intends you to be? If you'll dare to take charge of your life and be disciplined in your thoughts, your feelings, your emotions and your actions, God will take you to places you've never dreamed of – and you'll live the life of victory He has in store for you.

Choose to Hope in God

Living a life of hope is a wise choice – and it's a wise choice because we have a strong and faithful God. So many people today are depressed and discouraged because they only focus on their present circumstances, but we serve a God who makes all things possible!

The Bible says in Hebrews 11:1 that "faith is the substance of things hoped for and the evidence of things not seen." Faith allows us to hope for what we cannot see and believe that God is at work in our lives, even when our situation seems bleak.

The enemy wants you and me to think our present is impossible and our future is hopeless – but that is a lie! Satan will work overtime to convince us that all is lost. He'll tell you your marriage is never going to get any better. That it's impossible for you to get out of debt. That you'll never be healed of sickness or of hurt.

That your addiction will always control you. He wants to steal your hope and my hope because he is a thief and a liar, and the father of lies (John 8:44). But friends, if we're going to be the people God really wants us to be, we've got to live with an attitude of expectancy, knowing that God has much better things in store for us!

When God told Abraham that he and Sarah would have a child, Abraham knew in the natural that the situation was hopeless. He was old. Sarah was old. They'd never had a child in all the years before. But you see, Abraham didn't focus on the impossibilities. He didn't dwell on his present day circumstances. The Bible says he believed God, and God counted that belief to him as righteousness.

Abraham didn't allow the enemy to fill his mind with all kinds of fear, worry and doubt. No, he made the choice to look beyond his circumstances, and believe God would do what He said.

Romans 4:19-20 says, "He considered not the weakness of his own body nor the deadness of Sarah's womb. But against all reason for hope, he hoped on in faith."

Notice Abraham didn't consider his situation. He considered the promise and power of Almighty God. He chose to believe God and to put his hope in what God had told him.

Some of you today are standing at a crossroads. God has placed a dream in your heart. You know He has better things in store for you. But all your circumstances shout that you are a fool to hope. The enemy's telling you to give up and give in to despair. Maybe your friends are even telling you that you're just wasting your time. But you've got to choose hope. You've got to do just like Abraham did and go against the odds – hoping, praying and believing in God.

Quit considering your circumstances. Quit considering your past. Quit considering what you don't have and what you can't do. Look past your own education, your own natural ability, and your own resources. Quit listening to all the naysayers who say it's time to take matters into your own hands. And make the decision today to *start considering your God.*

Jesus said, "The things that are impossible with men are possible with God." You may well have obstacles in your life that are very high, but we serve a most high God. Your enemies may be powerful, but your God is all-powerful. He's the God that flung the stars into space. He's the God that spoke the worlds into existence. When He said, "Let there be light," light came in at 186,000 miles per second! That's power – and that's the God we serve. He's called *Jehovah Rapha,* the Lord our healer. He's *Jehovah Jireh,* the Lord our provider. He's *El Shaddai,* the God who is more than enough.

Friends, this great I Am, the creator of the universe, the almighty God is on your side today. And if God is for you, who can dare be against you? You see, you and God are a majority! The Bible says, "No man can stand against our God."

You might say, "Joel, you're just getting everybody's hopes up," and you know what? You'd be right. I am! Because I want to get your hopes up. Not in my words – but in your great and mighty God. Choosing to hope in Him is the wisest decision you'll ever make. If God can set you free from sin and death, if He can make you righteous in God's eyes, is there anything He can't do? If I can get you to raise your faith today and stop focusing on where you are, there's no limit to what God can do in your life. No limit! He loves you. He is for you. You are the apple of His eye and His arm is strong to save. He said, "You didn't choose me – I chose you." And friends, if you and I are chosen by God, is there anything to fear? Is there anything to dread? Is there anything He can't do when we put our faith and hope in Him?

The apostle Paul said in II Corinthians 4:17, "For our light affliction is but for a moment. And it works for us a far more exceeding and eternal weight of glory. For we don't look at the things which are seen; we look at the things which are not seen. For the things which are seen are temporary, but the things which are not seen are eternal."

Paul looked with the eyes of faith and saw himself as an overcomer. He focused on Jesus, the author and finisher of his faith.

The more you focus on your problems, the bigger they seem. The question before you today is whether you will magnify your problems, or magnify your God. The bigger you see your God, the smaller your problems will become. And the more you keep your eyes on Him, the more faith will continue to rise in your heart. Look beyond where you are right now – because friends, if you can see the invisible, God will do the impossible. Don't consider your circumstances. Consider your God. Choose hope, and you'll live the abundant life that rightly belongs to you.